CONTENTS

WHAT IS POLLUTION?

Pollution happens when something **contaminates** its natural surroundings. We call something that pollutes an area, a pollutant. Pollutants are usually waste materials.

There are many different types of pollution, some of which we shall explore in this book. Pollution causes negative changes to be made to the environment, which can affect our lives and the lives of the animals around us.

AIR POLLUTION

Air pollution is the most dangerous type of pollution because we breathe it in. Air pollution usually occurs when a fuel is burned and releases harmful chemicals into the air.

Smoke from chimneys, factories, vehicles and fires are all air pollutants. When rubbish is burned, the chemicals released into the air cause pollution. That is why it is important for us to reduce the amount of rubbish we create by reusing and recycling.

Everyday activities such as driving and cooking, cause air pollution.

ASTHMA

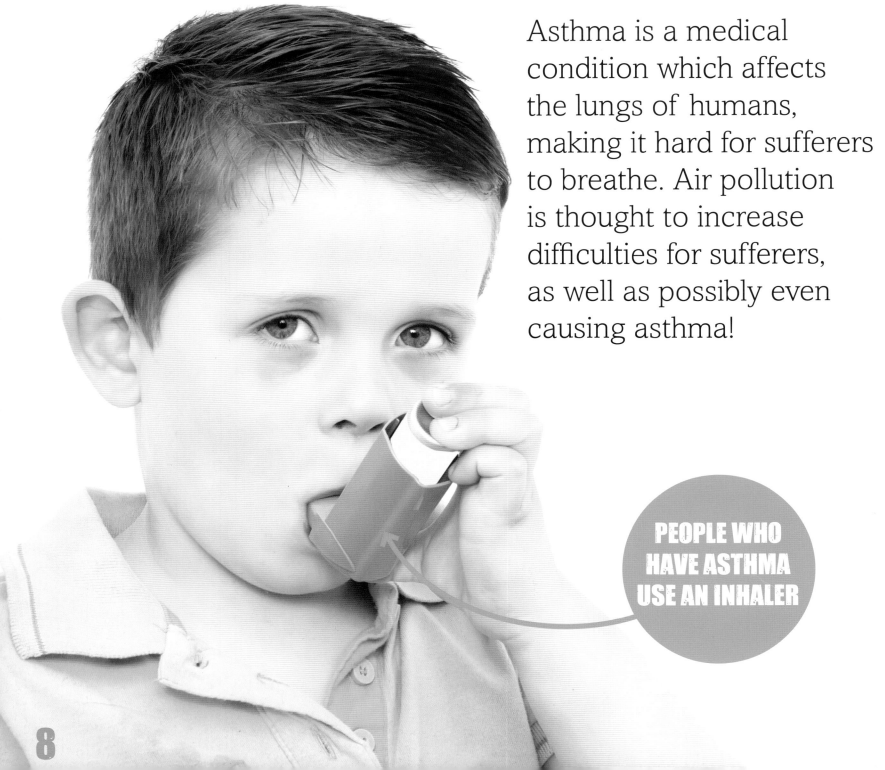

Asthma is a medical condition which affects the lungs of humans, making it hard for sufferers to breathe. Air pollution is thought to increase difficulties for sufferers, as well as possibly even causing asthma!

PEOPLE WHO HAVE ASTHMA USE AN INHALER

ACID RAIN

When the air is heavily polluted, the pollution can get into the rain that falls back down to Earth. Polluted rain is called acid rain.

Did you know that acid rain is dangerous for plants and animals and can cause them to die?

WATER POLLUTION

Water pollution is when our seas, rivers and lakes are polluted. Water pollution can be caused by acid rain. It can also be caused by oil spills and **industrial** wastes being dumped into rivers.

Water pollution has a huge impact on many **species** that live in or on the water. Many fish and animals become ill and die because of water pollution. Even humans can be affected, because they eat fish which may have been poisoned.

OIL SPILLS

Oil spills at sea are generally far more damaging than those on land, because they can spread for hundreds of miles on the water. Oil spills on land are far easier to contain to one area.

SEABIRDS, FISH, MAMMALS AND SHELLFISH, CAN ALL BE KILLED BY OIL.

DIRTY WATER

Litter which finds its way into the sea is a type of water pollution. Litter can also be harmful to sealife. Sea turtles can mistake plastic bags for jellyfish and eat them, causing them to **suffocate**.

HEAT AND LIGHT POLLUTION

Heat pollution is due to an **excess** of heat in the environment. It increases the temperature of Earth and has been linked to **climate change**.

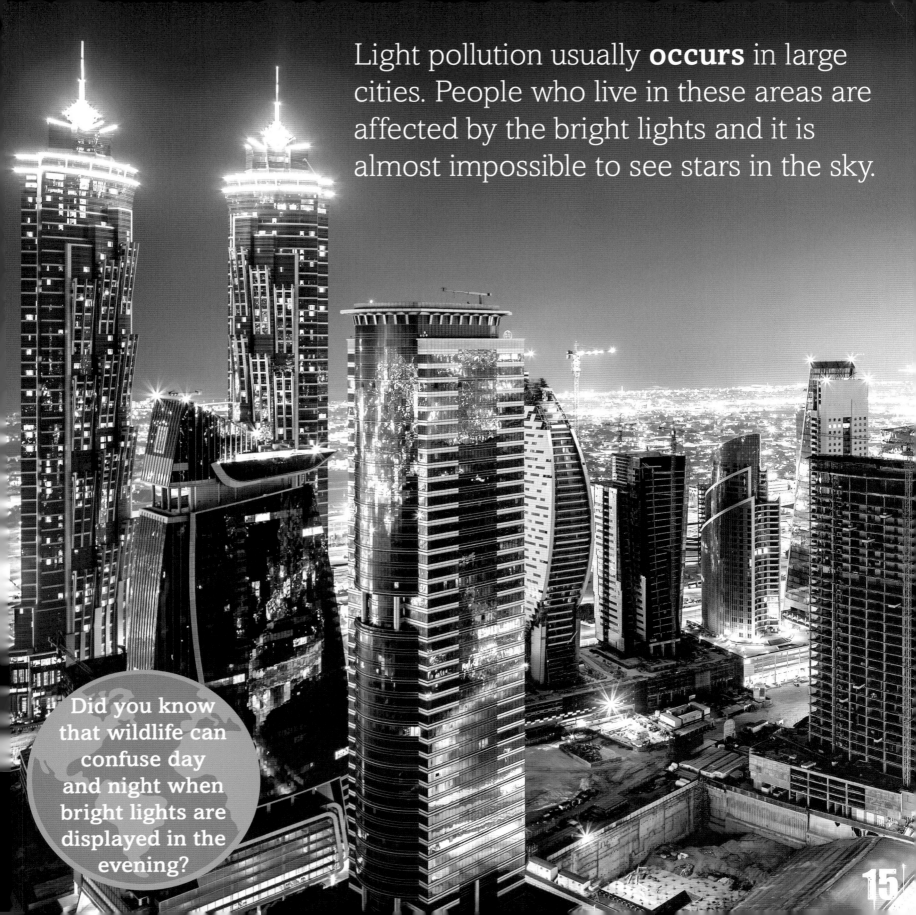

Light pollution usually **occurs** in large cities. People who live in these areas are affected by the bright lights and it is almost impossible to see stars in the sky.

Did you know that wildlife can confuse day and night when bright lights are displayed in the evening?

15

NOISE POLLUTION

Noise pollution happens when too much noise has a negative effect on humans or animals. Noise pollution is usually caused by machines or vehicles. Unwanted noise can cause **sleep disturbance**, hearing problems and high stress levels for humans.

LOUD NOISES CAN CAUSE TROUBLE SLEEPING

Noise pollution can also cause problems for wildlife. Too much noise can stop animals communicating with each other, making it difficult to hunt or breed.

SOIL POLLUTION

Soil is extremely important because it is where plants grow. We need soil in order to live, but soil can become polluted too.

WE NEED SOIL TO GROW PLANTS.

Soil mostly gets polluted by chemicals that man uses for **industry** or farming. Sometimes, accidents can cause soil pollution, such as stored oil or chemical leaks.

Since much of the food we eat grows in soil, it is possible that humans could be made ill by soil pollution. Plants are not able to grow as well in soil that is not healthy.

SOIL POLLUTION

FAILED CROPS

HUMAN ILLNESS

LITTER

Litter is waste that is dropped onto the ground, rather than put into a bin. Litter is a form of pollution because it can affect humans, animals and the ground below.

Litter is very untidy and can spoil the way a place looks. It can be dangerous to animals because they might eat or get trapped in the litter.

LITTER IS HARMFUL TO ANIMALS.

Even though it is bad for the environment, some people still choose to drop litter!

HOW CAN WE HELP?

There are a number of things that each of us can do in order to improve the level of pollution in our world:

CHOOSE TO WALK OR CYCLE, RATHER THAN TRAVELLING IN A CAR.

ASK THE ADULTS YOU LIVE WITH TO ONLY USE NATURAL PRODUCTS AROUND THE HOME AND IN THE GARDEN.

NEVER DROP YOUR LITTER ON THE FLOOR, IF YOU CAN'T FIND A BIN THEN TAKE IT HOME.

TURN LIGHTS OFF WHEN YOU LEAVE A ROOM.

WHY NOT ARRANGE WITH AN ADULT AND SOME FRIENDS TO PICK UP THE LITTER IN A LOCAL FIELD OR PARK?

GLOSSARY

climate change a change in the weather or temperature of a large area

contaminates to make something unclean by adding to it

excess a large amount

industry/industrial large factories where things are made

occurs happens

sleep disturbance not being able to sleep well

species a kind or sort

suffocate be unable to breathe

INDEX

Photocredits: Abbreviations: l–left, r–right, b–bottom, t–top, c–centre, m–middle.
All images are courtesy of Shutterstock.com.
Cover – Chris DeRidder. 1 – M. Shcherbyna. 2 – M. Shcherbyna. 3t – TranceDrumer, 3b – Nuttapong. 4 – TSpider. 5 – Alexander Tihonov. 6 – Hung Chung Chih. 7 – Balu. 8 ¬ smikeymikey1. 9 – OPgrapher. 10 – Toa55. 11bg – BMJ. 11inset – cubephoto. 12bg – Mrs_ya. 12inset - fluke samed. 13 - Willyam Bradberry. 14 – kwest. 15 – Anna Omelchenko. 16l – 3445128471. 16r – Andrey_Popov. 17bg – Alan Tunnicliffe. 17inset – Alan Tunnicliffe. 18 – udra11. 19: tl – Ansis Klucis; tc – Kaspars Grinvalds; tr – Kaspars Grinvalds; b nito. 20 – Maciej Bledowski, 21 – David W. Leindecker, 22l – studioloco, 22r – avel L Photo and Video. 23bg – Monkey Business Images, 23inset – Pavel L Photo and Video.

ENVIRONMENTAL
ISSUES

BookLife

By Gemma McMullen

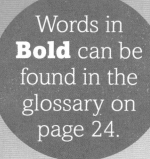

Words in **Bold** can be found in the glossary on page 24.

©2016
**Book Life
King's Lynn
Norfolk PE30 4LS**

ISBN: 978-1-78637-020-4

Written by:
Gemma McMullen

Designed by:
Ian McMullen

A catalogue record for this book is available from the British Library.